Aberdeenshire Library and Information Service
www.aberdeenshire.gov.uk/libraries
Renewals Hotline 01224 661511

ALI, Moi

Public relations

INFLUENCE AND PERSUASION

PUBLIC RELATIONS

MOI ALI

www.heinemann.co.uk/library
Visit our website to find out more information about **Heinemann Library** books.

To order:
☎ Phone 44 (0) 1865 888066
🖷 Send a fax to 44 (0) 1865 314091
💻 Visit the Heinemann bookshop at www.heinemann.co.uk/library to browse our catalogue and order online.

First published in Great Britain by Heinemann Library, Halley Court, Jordan Hill, Oxford OX2 8EJ, part of Harcourt Education.

Heinemann is a registered trademark of Harcourt Education Ltd.

Created, designed and produced for Heinemann Library by Trocadero Publishing, An Electra Media Group Enterprise, Suite 204, 74 Pitt Street, Sydney, Australia

Originated by Modern Age
Printed in China
by WKT

ISBN 0 431 09835 2
10 09 08 07 06
10 9 8 7 6 5 4 3 2 1

British Library Cataloguing in Publication Data
Ali, Moi
Influence and Persuasion: Public Relations – Creating an Image
659.2
A full catalogue record for this book is available from the British Library.

Picture credits
Airbus Industrie 20; Brand X Pictures 5, 6, 8, 10, 12, 14, 16, 18, 22, 24, 29, 30, 34, 35, 36, 37, 39, 43, 44, 45, 46 (top); Alamy Images/E. J. Baumeister Jr 46 (bottom); Comstock Images 9, 28, 32; Corbis/Gabe Palmis cover; Electra Collection 8, 40; Flat Earth Picture Gallery 6, 13; Getty Images/AFP 42; Newspix 21; Newspix/Leon Mead 27; Newspix/Peter Barnes 51; Newspix/Andy Baker 52; Oronsay Imagery/ Scott Brodie 9, 19, 25, 31, 33, 38, 41, 49; Popperfoto 23; US Army 19; World Health Organization/P. Virot 50

contents

introduction

There are many ways to influence and persuade. Advertising is probably the most blatant and familiar form of persuasion. Buy this. Drink that. Wear these. Drive one of those. Advertising is not the only force working to change how you think, what you wear, what you eat, and how you lead your life. Public relations, or PR, exercises a much more subtle, and arguably more powerful, influence over everyday life.

We are bombarded with advertising and we know its game. Nearly half a century ago, American sociologist Vance Packard wrote his million-selling book *The Hidden Persuaders* which exposed the advertising industry's tricks and techniques. Packard revealed how advertisers use psychological manipulation to get the public to buy anything from cake mix to cars. Although advertising undeniably continues to be hugely powerful, people are more sceptical these days. Advertising has to work much harder to get a result.

PR uses a variety of techniques to bring us to a particular viewpoint, to persuade us to change our behaviour, to encourage us to take (or not to take) a certain action. This often invisible force is working 24 hours a day, for good and bad, at home and abroad. It is changing how we think about charities, companies, causes, and campaigns.

This book explains what public relations is, who undertakes it, what methods it uses, and to what effect. Using real-life case studies, it shows how PR can be used to benefit society. PR techniques can promote healthy eating, highlight injustices, or keep

employees informed and motivated. Unscrupulous people use PR techniques to conceal the truth, to put a "spin" on things, to obscure the debate, to whitewash, mislead, and misinform. That is where PR ends and propaganda begins.

In the book you will find out about different branches of PR – public affairs and lobbying, internal communication, media relations, corporate social responsibility (CSR), and more – and what they involve. When you reach the end of the book you will be more PR-savvy, more aware of who is trying to influence you and for what end. You will be wise to the tricks of the spin doctors, and able to work out what is substance and what is spin.

Public relations is the art of spreading information about a product, an event, a person, or many other things. The PR professional is an expert at getting a client's image favourably presented to as many people as possible, as efficiently as possible.

what is public relations?

Most people think that PR is simply the art of attracting good publicity. However, there is more to it than that. One professional body that represents the PR industry is the Chartered Institute of Public Relations (CIPR). It defines PR as "the planned and sustained effort to establish and maintain goodwill and mutual understanding between an organization and its publics". Other PR associations describe PR in a similar way.

It is important to unpick the definition to find out what it really means. "Planned and sustained" means that PR is not a one-off activity but instead a carefully thought-out and ongoing programme. "Mutual understanding" is another way of saying that PR is a two-way street. It is not just about organizations pumping out messages and trying to influence; it is about listening as well, and making sure that the organization itself is open to the influence of others.

Old-style PR used to mop up the mess after a problem occurred. Modern PR helps organizations anticipate and avert problems. The main job of PR is to manage reputation. Some wrongly believe that this means trying to make people think well of an organization regardless of its faults.

When PR techniques are used to exaggerate the good and downplay the bad, or cover up shortcomings, it is known as "spin". Real PR is about helping an organization to be the best it can, not just saying that it is the best even when it is not.

PR people must cast a critical eye over their organization's practices, policies and procedures, highlighting weaknesses that could damage reputation. If they discover, for example, that their company provides poor after-sales service, their role is to ensure that this is addressed before it harms the company's reputation.

PR is sometimes considered to be a branch of marketing, although it is not. Marketing focuses on the four "Ps" – product, price, place, and promotion. A product is developed at the right price for the market, distribution is organized to get the product in place (in shops, for example), and promotional activities (advertising and so on) let people know about the product, how much it costs, and where to buy it. Confusion arises around the fourth P: promotion. PR professionals sometimes do

The Father of P.R.

Edward Bernays (1891–1995) is the so-called "father of public relations". Born in Vienna, Austria, and a nephew of the psychoanalyst Sigmund Freud, he was brought up in the United States. There he developed techniques to use in public persuasion campaigns. These combined his uncle Sigmund's theories of psychoanalysis (the analysis of the way the mind works) with psychology and sociology. He was the profession's first theorist.

"Publicists" existed before Bernays. Their job was to create positive publicity for travelling circuses and theatrical events. One of the best known was the 19th century's B.T. Barnum of the famous Barnum and Bailey's Circus, who billed his show as the greatest on earth. Today, publicists are employed to promote movies, books and CDs, and to boost the careers of their showbiz clients through positive media coverage.

Bernays was different in that he did more than simply attempt to attract positive publicity. He developed theories about how to influence people and shape their thinking. In this way, he turned PR into a science. He set out his ideas in a number of influential books, including *Crystallizing Public Opinion* (1923), *Propaganda* (1928), and *The Engineering of Consent* (1947). Bernays founded the United States' first PR consultancy, known as Edward L. Bernays, in 1919. Before that he worked for the US Committee for Public Information, or the Creel Committee, where he helped promote and win acceptance for the USA's emerging pro-war stance during World War One.

product promotion work, such as sending out press releases about new products. But promotional activity in marketing usually refers to paid-for advertising on TV, radio, and in the press, mailshots and other marketing publicity, such as point-of-sale material.

Responsibilities

PR involves a broad range of responsibilities, including:

Attracting positive coverage in the media

Avoiding negative media coverage

Monitoring and evaluating media coverage

Managing issues and crises

Communicating with employees to keep them informed and motivated

Promoting an organization's mission and values, both internally and externally

Promoting a positive image with various stakeholders, such as investors, regulators, governments, and others

Writing and producing publicity material

Looking after the organization's corporate identity and ensuring consistency of design

Supporting community activities and taking a lead on social responsibility

Managing events

It is better to think of PR as a fifth P, standing for perception, or the way that people look at a product or company. A great product at the right price will simply not sell if people have a poor view of the company making it. By taking care of an organization's reputation, PR shapes people's views, and creates a friendly environment in which the marketing people can do their job.

The PR industry today

The PR industry has changed since its early days. Today, it is larger, more sophisticated, and has more techniques at its disposal thanks to new technology. It is also no longer dominated by big business. At first, PR was usually only used by large companies, and it is true that the larger organizations continue to hold the biggest budgets for PR work. But today, hospitals, charities, small businesses, educational establishments, and a wide range of other organizations employ PR people or engage a PR agency to represent them.

There is a clear career structure in the industry, and academic courses are training PR graduates and postgraduates to work in this field.

Right up until the end of the 20th century, a significant number of PR consultants came with a background in journalism. As the focus of PR had for so long been media relations, it was useful to know how the media worked, making journalists the obvious candidates for PR jobs. That has changed. Placing positive stories in newspapers, and on TV and radio, is just one element of PR. Others include internal communication (with staff) and external communication using publications, events, exhibitions, corporate videos, websites, and so on.

Then there is lobbying and campaigning. PR has become more strategic and wide-ranging. Journalists are no longer automatically the best for the top jobs. Increasingly, employers look for someone with both practical and theoretical knowledge of all aspects of the PR business. This gives PR graduates a head-start.

PR is used by numerous organizations, including big business, hospitals, agriculturalists, and miners.

the business of PR

The founding father of PR, Edward Bernays, set up the first PR agency in 1919. Other consultancies followed, in the US and the UK. Today, there are literally thousands of agencies across the world. Over the years, larger consultancies bought up smaller ones, and a few players now have transatlantic and even global PR empires.

Porter Novelli, for example, has 102 offices spanning 60 countries. Hill & Knowlton has 72 offices in 38 countries. Edelman has 39 offices and is the world's largest independently owned public relations business. Founder Daniel J. Edelman set up this last company in Chicago in 1952, and is still involved today. There are many small agencies as well, employing

Not the best form of PR! Public relations is most effective when the target is influenced but remains unaware of how it happened.

just a handful of people, and specialist consultancies who major in one subject area, such a healthcare, music and show business, sport, or high-tech PR.

PR specialisms

Gone are the days when PR meant media coverage. Today, PR has a wide range of specialist areas that include the following.

Internal communications

Specialists in this field deal with employee communication. Their role is to communicate with staff so that employees are up to date with their organization's news, They also operate two-way communication channels so that workers can communicate with management and vice versa. Effective internal communication can make staff feel valued and respected, and persuade them that their views matter. This can motivate the workforce, reduce absenteeism and industrial action such as strikes, improve time-keeping and productivity, and reduce staff turnover. Investment in effective employee communication can reward an organization. Company propaganda has the opposite effect. Staff who are ill-informed, or given company propaganda that does not have any basis in truth, mistrust management and may feel angry and resentful. Rising absenteeism, general unrest, and a fall in productivity often follow.

Effective communication techniques

Staff newsletters and written briefings

Intranets and electronic noticeboards and chatrooms

Staff meetings

Cascade briefings (managers are briefed and they in turn brief their immediate staff, who in turn brief the staff they manage)

Staff conferences and away days

Corporate videos

Print production

This involves managing the production of printed publications such as customer newsletters, brochures, and annual reports. People who work in print production draw up production schedules. They also oversee the various stages of producing printed publicity, from briefing designers and photographers to proofreading and liaising with printers.

Media relations

There are many elements to media relations. Relationships must be forged with relevant reporters, correspondents, and producers. Press releases must be issued and photo opportunities organized. The aim is to attract as much positive publicity as possible, and to avoid or minimize negative media coverage.

Crisis management

Crisis management specialists advise on how to avert crises. They also help companies deal with crises while they are happening, and with any aftermath. When a company does something wrong or illegal, this can cause huge damage to its reputation. Even when the company is not at fault, a crisis can sometimes damage their reputation, so it is important that it is handled correctly.

Crisis management specialists offer training so that company spokespeople deal well with TV and radio interviews. The specialists also prepare media statements and briefings, and can organize product recalls – if something is faulty, it may be called back to the factory. They can also set up helplines. In this way, they help shape the public's opinions of an organization in crisis, and encourage people to think well of the company.

The photo opportunity is a favourite technique used by PR practitioners to promote the image of a person or organization.

Government relations

This specialist area goes by various names – lobbying, public affairs, or government relations. Lobbyists are expert in how laws are made, debated, approved, and put into practice. They help organizations to influence public policy and political debate. This may involve persuading governments to reject, delay, or change planned legislation. It may be that they encourage a revision or an update of an existing law, or help introduce new policies.

Sometimes, the public or media are targeted to build support. Sometimes lobbyists work quietly behind the scenes, and the public may never become aware that a campaign has happened.

Lobbyists can campaign for public good, perhaps by representing pressure groups who wish to introduce stronger legislation that requires recycling and so protects the environment. Or they can operate in a more sinister way by secretly representing the vested interests of big business at the expense of public protection.

The form of PR known as lobbying employs thousands of people working to influence the decisions of governments and legislatures around the world.

people who work in PR

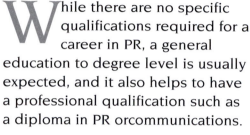

While there are no specific qualifications required for a career in PR, a general education to degree level is usually expected, and it also helps to have a professional qualification such as a diploma in PR orcommunications.

The qualities needed to be successful in PR include self-confidence, charm, and the ability to get on well with all kinds of people. But it is not enough simply to be a bright and breezy, good-looking individual with an immense ability to charm, despite the popular view that this is all that PR amounts to! An effective PR professional must be able to write well, in a variety of styles, to tight deadlines. They must also have presentation skills, and be able to plan and deliver impressive and confident talks and presentations to audiences large and small. They must be well organized, and able to manage the competing pressures on their time. And it is vital that they are creative and full of ideas.

A great deal of the PR person's daily work is office-based. PR practitioners must be well informed and up to date on all industry practice.

One of the myths of PR is that it is a glamorous career which involves lots of jet-setting, mixing with the rich and famous, and endless rounds of parties, lunches, and events. This may be the case for a few people working in show business PR, but the reality for the majority of PR people is far more ordinary.

Much of the PR person's work is office-based and involves reading, researching, and writing. They must be up to speed with the news and developments in their area of expertise, so they need to read relevant newspapers and magazines, monitor the right websites, and maintain contact with experts, key business people, and relevant journalists. Much of the contact with others is via the telephone and email. Face-to-face meetings supplement this and sometimes they use tele- and video-conferencing.

PR people may work in-house for a company, charity, government, hospital, or some other organization. They may work for a PR or marketing consultancy. Or they may operate independently as self-employed freelancers, working for companies when needed.

In-house roles

It is most common for PR people to work in-house, on their own, or as part of a larger PR team or department. No two organizations are the same, but a typical PR department will have a head of

People in PR come from all types of backgrounds. Typically, they are outgoing personalities with the ability to represent their clients' interests in the best possible light

department, one or more PR managers, PR officers, PR assistants, and a press officer. The role of the press officer is to handle calls and enquiries from journalists, issue information to the media, and try to secure positive news and feature coverage for the company.

Consultancy roles

A consultancy or agency is a firm that specializes in general PR, some aspect of PR such as lobbying or media relations, or a business sector such as consumer PR, B2B (business to business), or healthcare PR. Consultancies are organized into teams, and a team is responsible for handing an "account" – the business of a particular client (customer).

their services for an hourly, daily or project rate, helping businesses and organizations with their PR needs. They may also help in-house PR teams and PR consultancies when their services are needed.

Clients

People who work in PR sometimes face a dilemma. Their organization or client is paying them to promote that body's interests. In return for their money, they expect a good reputation to be built.

Although reputations take years to establish and a lifetime to maintain, those paying for PR want "quick wins" – they want to see clear benefits now, not next year. Sometimes the easiest way to get quick results is to exaggerate the good work that an organization is doing, or make untrue claims about its products and services. In the short term, such actions can lead to good publicity, but in the long term, misleading information damages reputation and can even destroy an organization. It is also against the ethical code to which most PR professionals subscribe.

So while PR activity must be conducted in the interests of the organization paying for it, it must also be done in an ethical way and in a way that protects the future reputation of the organization.

The account director leads the team, is responsible for strategy and may well have much of the face-to-face client contact. However, the account manager and account executives do the bulk of the day-to-day work on an account. Those working for non-specialist consultancies need to be able to learn fast: one week they might be working on fashion, and the next on fish or furniture.

Freelancers

A freelance consultant is self-employed. Some work from home, some from their own office away from their home, and some in their client's office. Freelancers offer

Regulation

In most countries, certain professions, such as medicine and dentistry, are protected in law and regulated (controlled) by government, Doctors and dentists working in these professions must meet certain minimum standards of education and training, and have to register for a licence to practise.

PR is not regulated. Anyone can call themselves a PR consultant regardless of their knowledge or experience. Someone thrown out of one of PR's professional bodies for bad practice can still continue to work in the industry.

In order to maintain professional standards and to build trust and confidence in the PR industry, the various PR bodies in Europe and North America each have their own formal code of conduct. This sets out the moral, ethical, and professional standards expected of members. If a member does not follow the code, a complaint can be made and an investigation will be carried out.

Different bodies have different policies on how to act following a complaint. The professional body may offer to mediate between the complainant and the member to resolve the problem, or it may offer advice and guidance to the member to help avoid future complaints. A member may be reprimanded, ordered to pay costs, or have their membership terminated.

Each professional body has its own code, but most require:

honesty and integrity

proper regard for the public interest

the use of only reliable and accurate information.

While professional bodies promote good practice, they can do little to make sure it happens. There is no one to inspect companies who do not voluntarily sign up to follow a code of conduct.

who uses PR & why?

Once PR was something that was used mainly by companies and business organizations. Now churches, hospitals, local and national government, charities, trade unions, universities, and other educational establishments have become PR-users. In the commercial world, small and medium-sized businesses also use PR. Royalty, celebrities, and other high-profile individuals, too, take PR advice and act upon it.

Why do they use PR? They use it because it works. Entrepreneur Richard Branson's Virgin Direct financial services company used PR techniques in order to attract media coverage to promote its launch in 1995. One of the stunts he used to obtain media exposure was to offer his leading competitor two upper-class tickets on Virgin Atlantic to anywhere in the world if this rival outperformed Virgin's new product. Branson found his investment in PR was more than 30 times as effective as money spent on advertising. People are more likely to regard a favourable article in the press as truly independent, whereas they know that advertising has only the interests of the advertiser in mind. Branson found that positive media coverage fuelled a word-of-mouth campaign. People are more likely to trust a recommendation from a friend than from an advertisement.

Major corporations rely on PR specialists to carry their messages to the public, government and their customers.

Anita Roddick, founder of The Body Shop chain of beauty and cosmetic stores, claims that her own high profile annually saves the company millions in advertising costs. Even though she no longer runs the business, it still benefits from her involvement. Roddick believes that positive media coverage is better than advertising at influencing people. She uses the Body Shop's unique selling proposition (USP) – the company's ethical and socially responsible stance – to get the media to talk and write about her and fix the company name in the public's mind.

Cola Wars

Entrepreneur Richard Branson maintains a high media profile thanks to a team of PR people who work up stunts to keep him and his products in the headlines. When newcomer Virgin Cola decided to take on market-leader Coca-Cola in the United States, Branson drove a tank up to the Coke sign in New York's Times Square and fired at it to launch the challenge. There was massive media coverage, worth thousands of dollars, and Virgin Cola was firmly on the map.

The Body Shop and Virgin are not alone. Starbucks, the coffee house chain, and Google, the Internet search engine, are among companies that rely on the power of PR to generate interest. Products such as the Harry Potter books and PlayStation 2 also experienced massive sales as much from PR efforts as from advertising. The activities of the PR specialists of Microsoft's rival to PlayStation, the XBox, created such a stir that 75 per cent of the target audience was interested in buying one even before the first ad appeared.

Major names such as The Body Shop and Virgin have used the personalities of their founders to raise the profile of the business. This has helped them become almost universally known, often around the world.

Individuals who use PR

In the past, individuals such as pop stars, sports personalities, and other celebrities, would use publicists to raise or maintain their profile. Now these people employ PR professionals to help shape the way their public think of them.

One way PR people help their celebrity clients to create a positive image is by advising them to support charitable ventures. Big names such at Britney Spears, Kylie Minogue, and Leonardo DiCaprio take part in events to raise money for charity, or help a cause close to their heart to raise its profile. No one would claim that celebrities' charitable works are only publicity stunts to enhance their profiles, but it is true that supporting the right kind of worthwhile cause can help shape their public image.

American style guru Martha Stewart used the media over many years to build her reputation and to influence everything from how fashionable Americans presented their homes to what they ate. Despite being convicted in 2004 of lying to investigators, conspiracy, and obstruction of justice – all related to her improper sale of shares on the stock market in 2001 – she continued to profit from media exposure. Although she did not testify during her trial, she appeared on many chatshows before, and arranged for friends in show business to come to court or speak to the media in her defence.

There is an old saying: "no publicity is bad publicity", and this certainly seems to be the case for Martha Stewart. As she strode from the court after her trial, a convicted criminal awaiting sentencing, people in the street chanted: "We want Martha!" A Save Martha website was also set up selling Save Martha tote bags, offering downloadable Save Martha posters, and providing a facility to send supportive emails via the website to the judge responsible for sentencing. Sales of Martha Stewart-branded goods in the US were strong in the lead-up to and following the trial.

While the popular view of PR is that it is about attracting publicity, infact it is not so much about publicity as about reputation. Therefore a comment that receives a lot of publicity can also damage reputation.

In addition to their talent, good PR can prove vital in enhancing the careers of actors. Russell Crowe and his wife pose for the cameras at a movie premiere.

Changing attitudes

There was a time when playing the PR game was regarded as undignified, particularly when it came to figures such as the British royal family. Buckingham Palace would refuse to confirm or deny media stories and they seldom sought publicity for anything other than public royal engagements.

That began to change a few years ago when the late Princess Diana moulded a positive public image with very clever use of the media.

Some apparently private mercy missions to the sick and dying were mysteriously tipped off to the media. They in turn carried coverage that was favourable to the princess and highlighted her caring and compassionate nature. Despite an upbringing of aristocratic privilege and immense personal wealth, Princess Diana shaped an image as the "People's Princess". She even used the media to expose the breakdown of her marriage, to portray herself as the wronged party, and to win public sympathy as a result. Stunts like this caused the more cynical media saw her as a devious self-publicist.

P.R., Gerald Ratner-style

British businessman Gerald Ratner would probably disagree with the statement that no publicity is bad publicity. Speaking at a business dinner he criticized the products sold in his chain of jewellery stores, stating among other things that some of the earrings he stocked were "cheaper than a prawn sandwich". When his ill-advised remarks were reported in the media, £500 million was wiped off the value of his company and collapse swiftly followed. The company's reputation as an affordable high street jewellers, which took years of positive PR to achieve, was lost overnight thanks to Mr Ratner's PR gaffe.

Princess Diana (left) with a group of ballet dancers at London's Sadlers Wells Theatre, at the height of her career as the "People's Princess". She constantly used PR to present herself and her causes in the best possible light.

The princess had PR advisers but she sometimes acted without first seeking their guidance, or she would ask for advice and then ignore it. Although she generally attracted hugely positive publicity, the negative stories were often the result of actions she undertook without the support of her PR people.

John Gummer

In 1990, the bovine illness BSE (bovine spongiform encephalopathy), or Mad Cow Disease, was in the headlines. There were public fears that the deadly disease could affect humans through the food chain.

This led the British government minister for agriculture, John Gummer, to feed his four-year-old daughter a hamburger at a photocall. He wanted to demonstrate his confidence that BSE could not be transmitted to humans.

Today, we now know that it can. People have since died horrible deaths from CJD, the human variant of the disease. Even at the time, when the science was uncertain, the minister was criticized for using his child for PR purposes, and the publicity probably affected his career.

better than advertising?

PR = #1

Public relations used to be the poor relation of advertising. Advertising paid higher salaries and had bigger budgets to spend. Now PR is fighting back. *The Fall of Advertising and the Rise of* PR by Al Ries and Laura Ries argues that "the advertising era is over". They state that a recent poll on the honesty and ethics of various professions put advertising executives near the bottom of the list, that what people think of the profession has a direct effect on whether the work they produce is believed. They go on to say that a recent survey of 1800 businesspeople by the American Advertising Federation (AAF) shows that PR is more highly regarded than advertising. PR may not actually be any better. The difference is that the hand of PR is harder to detect, so the public has more faith in what is said by a PR person than by an advertising executive.

Advertising is about control. An advertiser can say where an ad will appear, when and for how long. The content of the ad, too, is completely within the advertiser's control. So how can PR be more powerful?

Influencing car buyers

Imagine your parents are buying a new car. They might see an ad claiming that a particular company makes the safest and most reliable cars. Will they rush out and buy one of their cars as a result? No, because they expect ads to say good things about the product being advertised and they do not believe the ads. Next, your parents read an article in a national newspaper that compares the safety features of various cars. The car from the ad comes out top on both safety and reliability. Your parents believe the content of the press article because it was written by an independent journalist, an expert motoring correspondent, and published in a trusted and well-respected national newspaper. They are influenced and rush off to buy a car from the company.

What your parents do not realize is that the idea for the feature was fed to the journalist by the company's press office, who even flew him to tour the factory, take a test drive, and enjoy a little corporate hospitality.

No one is saying that there is anything corrupt or underhand here. It is perfectly legitimate for a car manufacturer's press office to suggest a feature on car safety to a motoring correspondent. It is also fine for them to organize a press trip to see the company's facilities and to try the products. However, the effect is that the journalist is

PR is a vital tool for motor vehicle companies wanting to influence people who are considering buying a new car. Items which appear in the columns of newspapers and magazines are much more influential than advertising.

influenced (which was the intention). The journalist in turn influences readers, which has a positive effect on car sales.

This string of events is known as the "third party" technique because the company is using a third party, the journalist, to promote their product.

media coverage advantages & disadvantages

Public Relations		Advertising
Cheaper – staff time & postage only	**cost**	Expensive – creative & production costs, space/airtime costs
No guarantees – could appear anytime or never	**certainty**	Guaranteed – you specify when & where
More credible – seen as third party endorsement	**credibility**	Less credible – people more sceptical of advertising
Widespread coverage possible in press radio & TV	**coverage**	Expense means coverage may be limited by budget
Left to journalist to interpret	**control**	You define the message

PR has acted as an invisible force, influencing and persuading. Advertising cannot sneak about undetected in this way. People might think differently about journalistic articles if they knew that many media articles come about as a result of PR agents courting journalists and sending out press releases. That is not to say that journalists are simply a channel for PR material. But PR material does reach them and they do use it. The source of the story – the PR expert – is camouflaged. The hand of PR is hidden.

Lobbying

Attracting positive media coverage is an important aspect of PR, but there are other ways of influencing. Lobbying is one of them, and it is used by companies, large organizations, charities, pressure groups, and individuals when seeking to prevent or influence planned legislation or amend existing legislation.

Specialist PR practitioners called professional lobbyists may be used to spearhead the lobbying. These experts know how the legislature works and many are on first-name terms with key politicians. Through their personal contacts and their knowledge of the system, they can help organizations get their message across to the right people, at the right time, in the right format.

Lobbying for the Sydney Olympics was tainted by claims that IOC members were given grants to fund sporting projects in their countries.

Over the years there have been concerns that lobbyists sometimes buy influence from corrupt decision-makers. While there are examples across the world of corruption, legitimate lobbying is important to the democratic process.

Lobbyists are not used only to influence legislature. They may also be hired to influence the outcome of decisions made by non-legislators, a good example being the lobbying of those involved in the Olympic Games.

While legitimate lobbying occurs, there are examples in recent times of corrupt lobbying too. Legitimate lobbying might involve building up profiles of the members of the International Olympic Committee, the IOC (who decide where the games will be held), in order to tailor a bid that will appeal to them.

This kind of intelligence gathering is quite acceptable.

Illegitimate lobbying can involve all sorts of underhand activity, including bribery and inappropriate payments. This is alleged to have happened when Australia hired a consultant who, it is claimed, gave two members of the IOC large grants to fund sporting projects in their own countries in order to help secure their votes for the Sydney games. There were also allegations of corrupt lobbying around the 2002 Salt Lake City Winter Olympics, as well as the forthcoming 2012 Olympics.

There is no place for PR in this kind of activity. PR seeks to influence by reasoned persuasion, not financial arm-twisting.

creating public confidence

Many people wrongly think that PR is mainly about achieving media coverage. This is an old-fashioned view. PR is not so much about producing yesterday's press cuttings today as about averting tomorrow's problems. PR people identify possible issues with an organization's products, policies, or procedures, and take preventative action to avoid negative coverage. It is always better to avoid problems than clean up the mess after a disaster.

Even so, crises do happen and most large organizations have well-crafted plans ready to put into action. By handling a crisis well, an organization can protect its reputation and calm public fears.

If the unexpected happens, the PR department or external PR experts will be drafted in to devise and work out a crisis recovery plan aimed at damage limitation and reputation regain. There is a whole crisis management industry that acts under the PR umbrella.

Salmon crisis

In 2004, the Scottish salmon industry was forced to launch a crisis management plan following the publication of a report by the University of Albany in New York State claiming that salmon farmed in Europe were contaminated with cancer-causing chemicals.

Scientists can play a key role in building public confidence, as they did for the Scottish salmon industry.

Claims that Scottish salmon was contaminated with cancer-causing chemicals were countered by a massive PR blitz which restored the public's confidence.

The aim of the crisis plan was to deny the allegations and reassure consumers of the health benefits of the fish. Scottish Quality Salmon (SQS), the industry body, had anticipated that they might be criticized. They had already devised a plan just in case. Through their PR agency, they issued 46,000 statements worldwide, paying particular attention to countries that imported Scottish salmon, such as France, Japan, and the USA. UK supermarkets and wholesalers were also targeted, press releases sent to trade press, and a leaflet produced for consumers.

The spokesperson selected by SQS to front media interviews was a scientist whose talent was to put forward scientific argument using clear language. This made him more appealing to the media and the public. The SQS also sought backing for their denials from the Food Standards Agency in the UK and the USA's Food and Drug Administration. Celebrity chefs such as Jamie Oliver offered their backing for Scottish salmon, Scottish salmon farmers were given advice on how to handle the media, and journalists were invited to visit salmon farms.

Through the swift actions of the PR team, a negative and hugely damaging story was turned around. Of the 280 newspaper stories and 150 broadcast items, half were positive at the start. This number rose to 80 per cent. The leading supermarket Sainsbury's reported that sales of salmon rose 9 per cent in the week after the damning report. Reports of healthy sales further helped to restore consumer confidence.

Tylenol

As this case shows, a crisis need not destroy a company, or indeed an entire industry sector. Effective PR can enable an organization to emerge not only untouched, but perhaps stronger.

The classic example of excellent handling by public relations is Johnson & Johnson's Tylenol crisis, which has gone down in PR history. In 1982, seven sudden deaths from cyanide poisoning in Chicago were linked to "laced" extra-strength Tylenol capsules. Some companies would probably have tried to calm fears by playing down the danger, or even have put financial concerns above public safety.

Johnson & Johnson used the media to alert consumers and the medical community. They recalled 31 million bottles of the product (with a retail value of US$100 million) and offered to exchange any of the product that had already been purchased, something that cost the company millions of dollars. They also cancelled all ads for Tylenol, and they temporarily halted all production and replaced the capsules with tamper-proof caplets. They also put up a reward of US$100,000 to help catch the killer who had tampered with the tablets.

This was the first time that a company had acted in this way in response to a crisis. Some people feared that such radical action would be more damaging to the company than a more low-key approach.

The action taken by Johnson & Johnson when its Tylenol headache remedy was threatened, is a textbook example of how good PR is conducted.

By the end of the crisis there had been nationwide panic, the company's share price had fallen, and sales of Tylenol had plummeted. Marketing experts said that the Tylenol brand, Johnson & Johnson's most profitable, was dead.

Sounds like a PR disaster, but it was far from that. Effective, open, and honest PR during the crisis, combined with swift action afterwards, including the introduction of a triple-seal tamper-resistant package – the first of its kind in the world – and giving millions of presentations on the reintroduction of Tylenol to people working in healthcare, meant that within a short time, Tylenol had recovered and even improved on its place in the market. The company was applauded for its socially responsible reaction to the crisis. They were given wide and positive press coverage.

Nuclear controversy

Nuclear power is controversial even when nothing goes wrong. At the Windscale nuclear site in England, a string of accidents had left it with a very poor image. British Nuclear Fuels decided that a good way to win public confidence in the plant would be to rename it. The name Sellafield was introduced in 1981 in what was seen by many as a vain attempt by PR people to disconnect the idea of the plant from accidents that had happened in the past.

PR attempts to soften the image of nuclear power in Britain proved disastrous.

A revamped visitor centre costing over £5 million opened in 1995, which the company admitted was based on the Walt Disney approach, with lots of exciting hands-on exhibits for children. The plan was that a new generation would know nothing of Windscale and nuclear accidents, only of Sellafield with all of its fun and games. A visitor book was removed when people began to write unfavourable things in it.

The company produced an education pack for schools, again in an attempt to win support from younger people, but this was dubbed "nothing more than classroom commercials" by the National Consumer Council. Local people hit back against the PR by establishing a website setting out some of the true facts about the company and its nuclear plant. The attempt to gain public confidence has not been a huge success.

Restoring public confidence after a crisis is a big challenge. A reputation built up over time can be lost in a second and may take years to regain. Sometimes the challenge is impossible. PR can help mould a positive image, but it cannot work miracles.

The campaign was successful and changed behaviour. As a result of the combined PR and advertising campaign, the use of condoms increased, so the spread of the virus was reduced.

Governments and pressure groups in other countries followed suit. In Tamil Nadu, for example, an advertising campaign was backed up with culturally relevant PR activities such as puppet shows, drama, and street theatre in rural areas where literacy levels were low. In the Philippines and in Thailand, humorous publicity stunts were staged to promote the use of condoms. More recently, China has focused in the need to use PR techniques to help people cope with the AIDS problem.

Public information campaigns

Public relations experts are asked to organize public information campaigns from time to time. In the 1980s, when the deadly virus AIDS was discovered, the UK government ran a massive advertising campaign to promote safe sex because the virus was often passed on through unprotected sex. This was backed up with a huge PR drive aimed at securing media coverage in target publications and distributing public information material.

In the 1980s massive campaigns were conducted to alert the public to the new epidemic of AIDS which was sweeping the world

Healthy promotion

In response to health concerns about the fat content of fast food, particularly burgers, McDonald's came up with a master stroke in 2004: they launched a healthy range of salads. Great PR– or was it? This move should have shown McDonald's in a positive light, leading the way in healthy fast food and happy to offer an alternative to fat-laden burgers. The problem was that some of the salads actually contain significantly more fat than some of their burgers, as described on McDonald's own website. So instead of positive headlines, negative press coverage was the result. This was a PR failure.

DASANI

Already an established and successful brand in the United States, Dasani bottled water was launched by the Coca-Cola company in the UK in 2004. The PR advice should have been that bottling purified London tap water would attract bad publicity. In the UK, the leading brands of bottled water are either natural mineral waters or natural spring waters. The UK market has no appetite for bottled tap water.

Despite being heavily criticized in the media, Coca-Cola was upbeat. Dasani's brand manager said at the time: "…it is better to be talked about than not talked about. This week's events have created significant awareness for Dasani." Coverage, yes, but at what cost to reputation? As its PR agency worked on a recovery strategy, the final blow for Dasani in the UK came a few days later when some batches of the water were found to contain higher than acceptable levels of bromate, a potentially harmful cancer-causing chemical.

This time Coca-Cola got its PR right. Despite there being no immediate health or safety issues, an urgent product recall was put into action and 500,000 bottles of water were removed from shops nationwide.

McDonald's learned from the experience. Later the same year, the company announced that it had slashed the salt content in chicken McNuggets by 30 per cent and lowered the fat content. The move was welcomed and positive headlines accompanied it. This time, it was a PR success!

how a PR campaign is created

At the heart of successful PR is planning, and the steps involved are not dissimilar to those taken in a military campaign. Creating a PR campaign from scratch involves many stages. The starting-point is to set objectives – campaign outcomes are specified. These could be a change in the law, for example, or a change in attitudes or behaviour of the target audience. Once clear objectives are set, a strategy can be worked out to achieve them.

An effective strategy identifies targets. Who must be influenced? What kinds of arguments are likely to persuade this group? Who will front the campaign? What sort of spokesperson will appeal to the target group? A campaign to encourage schoolchildren not to smoke would probably be unsuccessful if fronted by a scientist explaining the medical effects of smoking. More likely to hit the right note would be a pop star or other teen icon explaining how unattractive people are when their clothes, hair, and breath smell like an ashtray.

Consultation and regular meetings to plan strategy and discuss progress are essential to creating an effective PR campaign.

There are many things that need to be considered. What tactics should be used? Are there any allies? Are there any enemies, competitors, or people with an interest in seeing the campaign fail? How will they respond to the campaign? Are they likely to launch a counter-campaign? Will any material be required, such as badges, leaflets, a website or posters? How, when, and where will the campaign be launched? How long will it run for? How will success be measured? How much will it all cost? Who will be responsible for the various elements?

Strategic thinking

Any significant PR campaign will be based on a written strategy which takes into account all of the above. A senior member of a PR team or consultancy will probably write the strategy, but it will be based on the ideas of a wider group of people. Usually, there will be a team meeting to discuss a campaign, and to brainstorm and develop ideas. Material generated at this meeting may be incorporated into the strategy. A strategy produced by a consultancy will then be presented to the client for approval. Strategies from an in-house team may be discussed with an organization's managers or directors for authorization.

Increasingly, PR people do research to inform their choice of strategy.

Informal discussions are also effective in running a good PR campaign.

Often this research involves focus groups, a small gathering of people from the target audience. By listening to what the target group has to say, and by understanding how they think, a more persuasive case can be put together. The more information a PR expert has, the more successful the campaign is likely to be.

Many companies use performers and celebrities to promote them. This is particularly effective in reaching younger age groups.

How PR reaches its targets

Successful campaigns are carefully targeted. And the target will depend on the campaign. A campaign to change the law might target politicians – or it may target the public instead, using them to exert influence on the politicians. A campaign aimed at the public may be fronted by a celebrity in a bid to influence ordinary people. This is known as endorsement. By endorsing or putting their name to an issue or cause, the celebrity gives it credibility and helps win the support of others.

The media is one of the most used channels for reaching the target audience. Young people can be reached through teen magazines and music stations on local and national radio. Professions can be approached through their particular trade and professional publications. Captains of industry can be targeted through business titles. Special interest groups can be communicated with through their specialist publications. There are ways of getting the message to almost anyone.

The media is not the only communications channel. In recent years, the Internet has become an important route for reaching a global audience. Traditional methods like leaflets and posters remain valuable ways of getting to the target with the campaign message. Events, too, play a part. One of the best ways of spreading the message is via a word-of-mouth campaign. You are far more likely to listen to and give consideration to something a mate tells you than to something you read in a newspaper.

Organizing a campaign that gets talked about is really hard. There is so much noise out there, so many other people bombarding us with messages and seeking to influence us, that creating a campaign that stands out from the crowd takes real skill.

Evaluating a campaign

In the early days of PR, little effort was put into evaluating the success or otherwise of a campaign. Often quite crude measurements were taken when assessing a campaign – for example, newspaper coverage. A lot of newspaper coverage meant success and only a little was considered failure. Although some organizations still use this crude measurement, informed PR professionals understand that media coverage can carry bad as well as good messages. Positive news coverage will enhance the reputation of an

organization, while the same measurement of negative coverage will damage it. Sometimes it can be more valuable to keep a story out of the news.

The best way to evaluate a campaign is to refer back to the objectives – the list of things the campaign set out to achieve. If a campaign aimed to whip up excitement in order to boost sales of a new music CD, success may be measured in the CD's sales figures.

PR, propaganda, manipulation, & deceit

Although PR is about the management of reputation, it does a poor job of managing its own. People are quick to dismiss a company's actions as a mere PR exercise. "Spin–doctoring" and "hype" are frequently used to describe PR. Why has it got such a bad image? It is because too many organizations use PR to manufacture an image that is only superficial. PR is used to cloud or bury concerns, and to create positive stories to divert attention from bad practice.

PR and propaganda both try to influence our ideas, what we like, and what we buy, but they have different aims and use different techniques.

Propaganda

Some people believe that there is a fine line between PR and propaganda. This is not helped by the fact that the father of public relations, Edward Bernays, wrote a book called *Propaganda*, which appears to view PR and propaganda as one and the same thing. He wrote about manipulation and controlling minds as being legitimate, democratic activities:

"We are governed, our minds are moulded, our tastes formed, our ideas suggested, largely by men we have never heard of .... In almost every act of our daily lives, whether in the sphere of politics or business, in our social conduct or our ethical thinking, we are dominated by the relatively small number of persons ... who understand the mental processes and social patterns of the masses. It is they who pull the wires which control the public mind."

Today, PR and propaganda are rightly regarded as two very different things. Propaganda seeks to influence people or to promote a particular agenda, and that is why it may sometimes be confused with PR. It also uses PR techniques such as posters, leaflets, media coverage, slogans, and so on. But there the similarities end.

Mind control

To many people, the activities of the PR industry amounts to mind control. By this they mean that PR is designed to pressure people into thinking in a particular way, to change their behaviour and beliefs in in a way that will benefit commercial or government interests. Opponents of the work of PR consultants say that most people would continue to live happy and contented lives if they never heard the PR message, whether it benefited them or not.

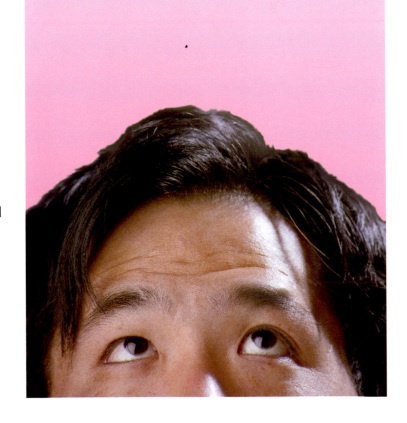

PR uses information to persuade and influence, whereas propaganda uses disinformation to deceive and confuse. It systematically presents biased information as impartial in order to mislead. Propaganda may leave out significant or vital information which, if known by the target, might cause them to think differently. Propaganda seeks to manipulate and to promote a particular religious, nationalist, or political doctrine or ideology. It may avoid the full truth, or falsify or distort the facts in order to achieve this. Usually only one viewpoint is presented and people are pushed into believing that there is only one way of looking at the issue.

Propaganda examples

Propaganda tends to be used in wartime, by some religious groups, or during times of political upheaval or change (such as during elections). Propaganda aims to subvert democracy.

PR is guided by a belief in honesty and integrity, a proper regard for the public interest, and the use of only reliable and accurate information. In this way, although it uses many of the techniques of

Nazi propaganda chief Josef Goebbels addressed crowds at the height of his powers in Hitler's Germany to spread his message of anti-Semitism.

Sydney Opera House in New York harbour? Unlikely, but a good example of the art of doctoring photographs to give a completely incorrect impression.

propaganda, and propaganda uses many of the techniques of PR, they are not the same thing.

One of the best-known and most devastating examples of the use of propaganda is Hitler's programme of anti-Semitism that killed so many Jews in Nazi Germany during World War Two. Josef Goebbels was a former journalist who became a German Nazi leader and a minister of Public Enlightenment and Propaganda in 1933. He used Bernays' book, *Crystallizing Public Opinion*, to help shape his campaign against the Jews.

Creating false impressions

New technology has resulted in a new propaganda technique: digital image manipulation. During the run-up to the US elections in 2004, a photograph of Senator John Kerry was deliberately altered in an attempt to discredit him. Photographs of Kerry were "doctored" so that he appeared to be at an anti-war event on the same platform as the peace campaigner and actress Jane Fonda. This could have had devastating consequences for Kerry's chances of selection as candidate, had not the attempted deception been exposed.

Although digital image manipulation is clearly a propaganda technique, it is one that is also used in PR. PR agents frequently issue to the media photos of their celebrity clients which have been manipulated to remove blemishes or to enhance their features. Even Bernays doctored photos as early as 1915, though not for any sinister purpose. He was PR adviser to the Ballet Russes when the Russian ballet company toured the USA in that year. He was lucky enough to get media coverage for his client in *Ladies' Home Journal*, but the magazine explained that it was unwilling to use photographs because they showed dancers with skirts above the knee. At Bernays' instruction, artists retouched the photos and lowered the offending hems!

The introduction of digital manipulation today has made this process both easier and more convincing. When the technique is used to enhance the beauty of someone in the limelight, it is PR. When it's used to damage the credibility of others or to create false events in an attempt to mislead, particularly in the political arena, it is propaganda.

Why are PR and propaganda sometimes confused?

Some PR departments use PR techniques to obscure or bury negative concerns. This is known as "spin doctoring" or "news management". It may involve releasing damaging information at a time when it is most likely to be missed or overlooked – such as over the quiet Christmas period – or deliberately issuing it just after the daily newspapers' deadlines have passed. With today's 24-hour news, the technique is less successful than in the past. This kind of activity is seen as underhand and gives PR a bad name.

North Korean dictator Kim Jong Il rules over his country as a dictator. The way the North Korean government manages its relations with the population is an excellent example of extreme propaganda.

Some PR consultants are described as "spin doctors". This is usually not very complimentary as such people are seen to be manipulators of the news or important current affairs. They are in the business of putting a positive "spin" on the activities of their clients, whether such activities are good or bad.

Some PR people are prepared to tell half-truths or even downright lies as they seek to manipulate rather than persuade by legitimate means. This is not PR; it is simply propaganda delivered by PR practitioners.

Front groups

It is not unusual for PR people to advise their clients: "Put your words in someone else's mouth." This is particularly when making controversial claims, such as "Smoking is harmless" or "Sweets do not rot teeth". A confectionery manufacturer claiming the latter would be laughed out of business. But if the same confectionery manufacturer teamed up with others to fund the Tooth Advisory Council, which claimed through its dentists that sweets are harmless to teeth, the claim might carry more weight.

It sounds far-fetched, but many industry groups do set up "front groups" to peddle their messages. These front groups are a deliberate attempt to deceive consumers by promoting messages favourable to big business. Meanwhile, they are pretending to be on the customer's side as impartial expert advice.

Trust me!

American Council on Science and Health

The American Council on Science and Health sounds like an official organization, perhaps connected with government. It describes itself on its website as "a consumer education consortium concerned with issues related to food, nutrition, chemicals, pharmaceuticals, lifestyle, the environment, and health." It states that it is an independent organization founded by scientists who were "concerned that many

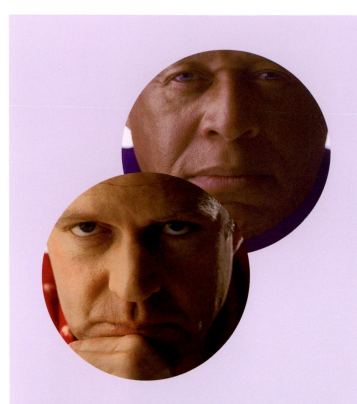

FORD: any colour but black

The Ford Motor Company found itself in trouble for doctoring photos in 1996. It was noticed that the company had changed black faces to white ones in a photograph of production-line workers used in an ad. The company superimposed white faces on those of four black workers and, when criticized, made matters worse by describing the incident as "an administrative error".

This action, and its poor handling of the resultant fallout, damaged the company's reputation with the car-buying public, as well as with its employees and trade unions. It is widely accepted in the PR profession that when an organization makes a mistake, it should admit the error and apologize profusely.

This example shows how bad handling by PR people can exacerbate an already bad state of affairs. Effective PR aims at easing a troubled situation, not making it worse.

important public policies related to health and the environment did not have a sound scientific basis. These scientists created the organization to add reason and balance to debates about public health issues and bring common-sense views to the public."

However, the American Council on Science and Health has been branded a "paid liar for industry" by the media, and has received funding from food and drinks companies, including Burger King, Coca-Cola, PepsiCo, NutraSweet, and Nestlé, as well as chemical, oil, and pharmaceutical companies such as Monsanto, Exxon, and Union Carbide.

The organization has defended petrochemical companies, the nutritional value of fast foods, and the safety of products that cause public concern, such as asbestos, saccharin, and pesticides. It is monitored by www.prwatch.org, a website which keeps a close eye on some of the more unsavoury aspects of the PR business. The website exposes supposedly independent experts and other spokespeople funded by the industry to manipulate the public's trust.

Corporates social responsibility

Corporate social responsibility (CSR) sounds like a great idea. A company does things to improve

CSR

Many invest in CSR not because they have good intentions, but because they are interested in what they can get out of it.

Research shows that companies successfully using CSR can benefit from greater consumer loyalty. They also have a better image, a stronger and more positive brand, increased sales, and an improved share price. Three in four people in the UK say that more information on a company's social and ethical behaviour would influence their purchasing decisions. Twenty per cent in the same survey admit to boycotting or selecting goods on social grounds.

the community in which it works. It also aims to trade and make profits. At the same time it takes seriously its responsibilities to employees, business partners, customers, and society at large.

Many large companies have CSR programmes, particularly those in controversial industries such as oil, mining, and tobacco. Does this mean that they are good, ethical, and caring enterprises? Not necessarily.

Scientists, with their positive public image, are often used by front groups to push a particular concept which is favourable to the clients of those groups.

An example of CSR would be if a drinks company's sponsorship of community projects is aimed at helping people with alcohol addiction. By supporting such schemes, and encouraging moderation in the consumption of alcohol, the company could be seen to be socially responsible. This would win over the public, and might encourage more people to buy the company's brand rather than that of a competitor's.

Do CSR programmes promote genuine social responsibility or do they deliberately manipulate us? Is a chocolate manufacturer being socially responsible when it gives away free sports equipment to

Some food manufacturers attempt to enhance their brand name by associating it with healthy pursuits such as sport. In fact, the food they are selling is often contributing to obesity or poor dental health.

schools in order to encourage fitness and health? Or is it merely exploiting young people by promoting itself as interested in fitness when in reality its products contribute more to the problem of childhood obesity and poor dental health than any other? Is it tricking people into buying more chocolate, not less?

Many shoppers are now demanding that retailers make a clear statement of how they see their CSR, or corporate social responsibility. This includes only selling merchandise which is manufactured or grown under fair and humane conditions and with environmental sensitivity.

Greenwashing

Some companies engage in "greenwashing"– that is, presenting themselves as caring, environmentally friendly, or socially responsible when in reality they are not. By supporting a few worthwhile, high-profile projects, they appear to be good citizens. This is mere window-dressing designed to deceive. CSR programmes should not be a shortcut to a good reputation. Good reputations lie in being a responsible company, not just pretending to be one. Effective CSR would need a company to take action to stop unethical practices. For example, certain companies would need to stop using child labour to make their goods, withdraw their support for a repressive regime, avoid polluting the environment, or pay good rates of pay to their staff. On top of that, such companies would need to make positive contributions to the society of which they are a part.

There are examples of genuine CSR. The Co-operative Wholesale Society in the UK takes its social responsibilities very seriously. In its supermarkets it sells a wide range of Fair Trade products. These are products such as coffee, sugar and fruit for which the Third World farmers who grew them were paid a fair price. All of its own-brand chocolate bars and coffees are Fair Trade certified. This is just one of many CSR initiatives run by the Co-op.

The controversy over genetically modified (GM) agricultural products has seen growers engage in campaigns to win a positive image for their crops.

Fair trading?

In 2004, Starbucks appointed a PR agency to run a campaign promoting the message in the US that it buys all its coffee in a socially responsible way and is committed to Fair Trade. Although the company had sold Fair Trade coffee since 2000, most of its coffee is not produced under fair trading conditions. The PR campaign was in response to criticism from consumers and pressure groups that therefore the company was not committed to fair trading. The only way to convince the public is for the company to significantly increase the amount of Fair Trade products that it sells.

A PR campaign alone, without action, is mere greenwashing. Recent reports have uncovered too many instances of CSR being used for cynical manipulation. "Behind the Mask", a report made in 2004 by the charity Christian Aid, concludes that CSR is a "completely inadequate response to the sometimes devastating impact that multi-national companies can have in an ever-more globalized world – and that it is actually used to mask that impact."

Despite the promotion, the impact of CSR is patchy, and those that claim to work in this way do not do so efficiently. One Harvard Business

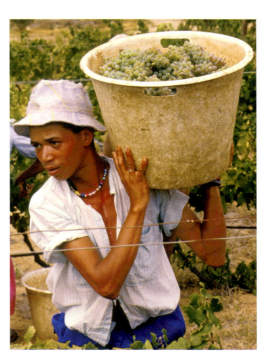

Fair trading is a system under which food growers in Third World countries can be assured of a fair price for their crops. The merchandise is then branded with a "Fair Trade" certificate so that consumers know they are supporting an ethical system..

School professor has described CSR as "a PR game".

A pressure group forced Virgin Group to rework the job description when they advertised for a CSR programme manager. In 2004, Virgin had looked only for applicants with experience of PR or marketing. It was felt by some that the role was not really about social change, just about giving the company a positive profile.

The Christian Aid report highlights the Shell oil company and its activities in Nigeria, which have brought no real gain for the many people who should have benefited. Shell's so-called "community development" programmes created a school, a hospital, and a village post office. Yet the school has never taught children, the hospital has never treated patients, and the post office has never handled a letter. Shell has failed to quickly clean up oil spills that ruin villages around the oilfields.

Shell has won awards for its CSR work, including an environmental award from Keep America Beautiful. Christian Aid claims that the reality "is a story that stands in stark contrast to Shell's professed commitment to 'core values of honesty, integrity and respect for people'". According to the Christian Aid report, Shell's interest in CSR came only after they realized that they had a poor public image. The share price fell following accusations that they were failing to meet their environmental and human rights responsibilities.

The Shell Company has come in for widespread criticism over its activities in Nigeria

Other global enterprises are also singled out by the charity. They say that Coca-Cola, for example, claim to use natural resources responsibly, yet one of their subsidiary companies in India is accused by Christian Aid of depleting village wells in an area where water is extremely scarce. Of course Christian Aid is a campaigning organization with its own agenda – one that is sometimes at odds with the objectives of big business.

Most large food and drinks manufacturers have CSR policies that are aimed at giving them a healthy image. Sport in particular gains from this. For example, sport in the UK received around £40 million in 2003 from the food, confectionery, and soft drinks industries. McDonald's and Coca-Cola both support grassroots football, Nestlé supports community tennis, and Kellogg's backs amateur swimming. These CSR activities do produce some good in that they are a source of funding and equipment that might otherwise not be available to local communities. But there is a concern among some health campaigners that their support of healthy activities is an attempt to deflect criticism from the fact that the products themselves are unhealthy.

Activism and pressure groups

Some organizations operate in an underhand way, presenting a good image while guilty of doing something unethical. In democratic countries, there is usually a pressure group somewhere trying to expose these companies' flaws. Sometimes these pressure groups are a band of amateurs with no money, fighting against a big corporation with a slick PR machine and expensive lawyers.

A good example of this is the so-called McLibel trial, in which the McDonald's burger chain sued activists Helen Steel and Dave Morris. They were two people who handed out leaflets outside a London burger bar claiming that the company exploited children with its misleading advertising, were

A Coca-Cola subsidiary was accused by Christian Aid of excessive water usage which was depleting natural wells in India, where water is often scarce or difficult to obtain.

Pressure groups can be very good at using PR to their advantage. It is especially effective when a movement can be characterized as the small person taking on a corporate giant. In this case it was against uranium mining on lands sacred to Australia's indigenous peoples.

responsible for cruelty to animals, and paid their workers low wages.

Even though it was found that McDonald's had been libelled, the lawsuit backfired and was a PR disaster for the company. McDonald's were seen by the public as big bullies using their wealth and power to silence two committed campaigners. The trial led to an anti-McDonald's backlash and the setting up of the highly critical McSpotlight website. This exposes McDonald's practices and accuses the company's PR machine of issuing propaganda disguised as factual information. The website gets one million hits a month.

It is not unusual for big corporations to use their immense muscle to silence those who speak out against them. In the 1960s, the American activist Ralph Nader decided that consumers needed information so that they could make informed decisions. His mission was to provide this information and his book U*nsafe at Any Speed* exposed potentially lethal design flaws in one of General Motors' cars, the Corvair. When GM tried to silence Nader by using PR muscle and hiring private investigators to scrutinize his private life with a view to undermining his credibility, law graduate Nader sued the company for invasion of privacy and won a huge out-of-court settlement. He went on to fight many more consumer campaigns, and is still active today.

Targeting footwear

One target of grassroots activism is Nike, the footwear and sports clothing manufacturer. In the 1996, a CBS television news programme exposed Nike for making staff at its Vietnamese plant work in very bad conditions for very bad pay. Nike disputed the claims but a number of pressure groups did not believe Nike.

According to the Washington DC-based Vietnam Labor Watch's Boycott Nike website, Nike decided that rather than tackle the poor working conditions it would staff up its American PR department "to go on a charm offensive to seduce the public, to create confusion among concerned people about the reality of Nike sweatshops and to sow doubts about anti-sweatshop activists. It now tries hard to look like a responsible citizen; it has put out more Nike-funded 'studies' and propped up Nike-funded organizations to be apologists for the Nike globalization agenda."

Marc Kasky, a community activist, sued Nike for conducting a deceptive PR campaign on this issue. In 2002, the California Supreme Court ruled that a company can be found liable for misleading public statements in press releases and letters to the editor. However, the court did not address either the truth or falsity of the claims made by Nike in its PR campaign.

Nike, the large sportswear manufacturer, has been targeted by pressure groups over working conditions in the factories where its products are manufactured in Vietnam.

In 2003, Nike settled the lawsuit by donating US$1.5 million to a labour monitoring group, the Fair Labor Association. The whole event started a debate in the world of public relations about corporate honesty and free speech.

Today's activists are becoming increasingly professional. Many campaigning organizations have PR departments. They even use PR consultancies to advise on techniques and tactics. The Internet has meant that pressure groups and even campaigning individuals have the same kind of presence, at least in cyberspace, as the huge global enterprises.

Public benefit or private advantage?

Is PR something that is undertaken for public benefit or for private advantage? The answer to that question is: Both. Some PR campaigns are undoubtedly run for social good. For example:

A government public information campaign to educate children about the dangers of smoking, to publicize the early signs of bowel cancer to adults, or to promote healthy eating for all

A charity publicity campaign to highlight the needs of terminally ill children in order to raise money for their care

A PR campaign to consult on a city's regeneration plans, and encourage local neighbourhoods to have their say in shaping the proposals contained in the final blueprint

A pressure group campaign to expose the unethical practices of a company and to use public pressure to exert influence on the company to change its ways

Clearly all of the above are PR campaigns that serve society. But not all PR campaigns are beneficial.

Take the first example, the campaign to educate children about the dangers of smoking. Such campaigns do happen. However, they are always countered by PR campaigns spearheaded by the tobacco industry and pro-smoking organizations.

Campaigns run by organizations with a vested interest are more likely to be one-sided and concerned with their own interests. PR campaigns that deliberately deceive are not in the public interest.

Many PR activities are neither for nor against the public interest. These might include:

A publicity tour to promote a pop band's new single

A stunt to attract attention for a new television series

A PR campaign to launch a new computer game

There is nothing wrong with companies using PR techniques to boost their profits, so long as they are driven by honesty and integrity.

detecting the hidden hand of PR

The most successful PR is often invisible. But how can you detect something that you cannot even see? It is not easy, but there are things to look out for, telltale signs that can help you to spot the hidden hand of PR.

One of the easiest ways of detecting a PR attempt to influence you is by analysing the media. PR tries to shape people's thoughts and actions by influencing the news agenda. Collect a pile of different newspapers containing the same day's news. Look out for stories that seem to be covered across most of the newspapers in front of you. Does the coverage use many of the same phrases and cover many of the same issues? Have two different newspapers carried coverage that uses very similar or even identical wording?

Make a note of the organizations that are being written about. They may be government departments, companies, charities, or some other type of establishment. Visit their websites and go to the online press office. You are likely to find the press releases that triggered off the media interest.

Some newspapers and other media are lazy. They accept the press release and reproduce it word for word. They may even add the name of their staff reporter so that the reader wrongly believes that the news report was generated by a journalist rather than a PR person. Most press releases include a quote from a company spokesperson. Compare the quote in the press release on the company website with the quote in the news report. Are they identical? If so, then you have exposed the hand of PR.

Soundbites

A technique that is easy to spot is the "soundbite'". A soundbite is a very short piece of TV or radio footage taken from a longer interview. It is a concise, newsworthy comment that can almost stand alone from the rest of the interview if necessary.

News editors look out for soundbites when putting together a short news package based on a longer interview. PR people have realized this and they coach spokespeople in how to construct a soundbite. Spokespeople may even be given a soundbite by the

Often a media release is copied without change by a journalist and published in a newspaper. It is then read by the public as if it were an original, properly researched article. The more ethical newspapers try to avoid this type of journalistic laziness.

PR team before they give a media interview so that they can practise. Some are shown how to deliver this rehearsed soundbite so that it sounds natural

Soundbites are also written into speeches that are likely to be broadcast or reported on by the media. Watch different channels and you will hear the same soundbite being repeated, particularly (but not exclusively) by politicians. "Axis of evil", "weapons of mass destruction", and "shock and awe" are examples of soundbites. These carefully crafted phrases were used by the USA's Bush administration as propaganda soundbites in the run-up to the Iraq war.

Distract and evade

Politicians are expert in a PR technique known as distraction or evasion. This is a way of avoiding answering a question without the listener noticing that they have not answered it.

The technique is taught during media coaching. Interviewees learn that it is not necessary to answer questions that are too probing or likely to make things worse for their employer or company. It is possible to skirt around the question, answering it with an upbeat, positive message which may have nothing to do with the original question. Listen to media interviews on TV and radio and compare the answers given with the questions asked. Look out for phrases like: "That's a really interesting point but what I'd really like to say is …". This kind of response indicates that the interviewee has been coached in media techniques by a PR person.

Counter-techniques

Public relations training also teaches counter-techniques. These are ways of helping make sure that a media interview is not broadcast. Interviewees use this technique when their organization is being grilled about a disaster or mistake that they would like to keep out of the public eye. By avoiding soundbites, and by rambling, using jargon, and so on, they make their response less suitable for broadcast. They also avoid saying anything memorable.

The written statement is another evasion technique. An organization submits a written statement to a TV or radio programme rather than supplying a spokesperson to answer questions. This again shows the hand of PR has been at work avoiding potential problems.

PR people are wordsmiths. They carefully select words in order to influence and persuade you to their way of thinking. You can see this most clearly when two opposing sides come head to head. For example, for a debate on genetically modified (GM) foods, a very specific vocabulary is used depending on the viewpoint of the person talking. An opponent of GM might describe the foods in media interviews, in printed publicity, and on websites as "Frankenfoods".

Distract and evade examples

Interviewer (to a politician)

"Your government has a very poor record of tackling illiteracy among adults, doesn't it?"

Politician

"It's really important that we focus on the huge investment we have made in literacy programmes over the last year. I should stress that our adult literacy campaign is among the best in the world ..."

OR

Interviewer

"Your new factory will destroy an area of outstanding natural beauty and create both noise and pollution. What do you have to say about that?"

Company spokesperson

"What you need to remember is that this factory will create much-needed jobs in the local community ..."

A supporter would choose words that sound positive, for example "natural" or "wholesome". Very different images are conjured up in each case. Constant repetition of these trigger words is another technique. Look out for it.

Slogans and logos

The slogan – a short, memorable catchphrase – is another way of getting across a PR message. Successful slogans catch on. This has the effect that many people end up communicating the message on an organization's behalf, thus increasing its impact. You can spot successful slogans on badges, T shirts, mouse mats, and mugs.

Logo placement, too, can communicate a message. Organizations being interviewed on TV will try to ensure that their logo is visible in the shot – unless the coverage is unfavourable. In this case, they take great steps to avoid their logo being seen.

PR people attending crisis management courses are taught that logos should be obscured or removed from crashed planes, sinking ships, burning factories, and other disaster sites if at all possible. They do this in a bid to avoid the logo being associated with misfortune.

These are some of the terms and techniques used by PR professionals around the world.

Using the Internet

The Internet is an excellent source of material for PR-spotters looking for alternative viewpoints to what organizations want us to know about them. Armed with information from both sides you can make up your own mind. Check out official websites. Then look at the so-called "sucks sites". These are set up by disgruntled customers. There are tens of thousands of such sites and the number is growing. For most large companies there will be at least one gripe site dedicated to unhappy consumers' experiences with their business.

Mass media attention first focused on these sites in 1995 when a Californian consumer set up www.starbucked.com to air his grievances about the coffee chain. The news was picked up right across the USA. Starbucks refused to enter the debate. Some companies responded by turning to the law to see if the site can be shut down. Others acted pre-emptively and bought up likely sucks site domain names such as www.ihateXYZcorporation.com, www.XYZcorporationsucks.com , andwww.XYZcorporationspotlight .com in order to make it harder for consumers to find any sucks sites relating to their enterprise.

Food labelling can be very complex. The conflicts between mass farming and smaller-scale organic agriculture are considerable. This leads each side to use words which are designed to put their products in the best possible light.

Pure frankenfood green wholesome natural

There are more learned websites, such as www.prwatch.com and www.infopaedia.com, that monitor the PR activities of the big corporations, governments, and PR agencies. They provide intelligent comment, useful background information, and sometimes eye-opening revelations.

So next time a PR campaign targets you, stop and think. Do not automatically accept what you are being told. Investigate for yourself. Gather information from other sources. Work out where any vested interest lies. Do not be manipulated. Make up your own mind – do not let others do the job for you!

The computer has become the major tool in the business of PR today. In particular, the Internet is widely used by PR organizations to get their messages across. It is also used by those who seek to counter the PR claims of large organizations.

anti-Semitism
An intense dislike of and prejudice against Jewish people.

campaign
Planned activities in order to reach a particular goal or outcome.

consultant
An expert who is called upon for a professional opinion or advice.

corporate
An association, company, or other body.

corporate social responsibility(CSR)
A company's efforts to trade profitably while also treating its employees, customers, society, and the environment with respect.

crisis management
Dealing with a crisis in such a way as to limit its negative impact on reputation.

democratic
A form of government in which the people make the decisions, or vote for others to make decisions on their behalf.

disinformation
Incorrect information issued with the express purpose of misleading people.

endorsement
A promotional statement in support of a cause or event.

ethical
The understanding of the difference between right and wrong; being ethical means making the decision to do the right thing.

Fair Trade
A system under which farmers who grow agricultural products in Third World countries are paid a fair price.

focus group
Originally a market research tool, a small group representative of a target audience is invited to discuss an issue. A focus group enables PR people to assess their opinions or responses to a particular subject.

freelancer
A PR person who works for him or herself rather than for an employer.

front group
An industry-funded group with a vested interest attempting to deceive the public. The group presents itself as an impartial source of expertise.

greenwashing
Supporting a few good causes in the environmental field in order to create the impression that a company is more caring, socially responsoible or environmentally friendly than it really is.

internal communication
Using PR techniques to enable management to communicate key messages to employees.

investor
A person who has shares in a company with a view to making a profit.

legislature
An officially elected or selected body of people with the power to make or repeal (cancel) laws.

libel
Write false, negative things about a person or organization, that are likely to damage their reputation.

lobbyist
An expert in how legislation is made. The lobbyist helps organizations to try and influence legislation in favour of or against a particular cause or viewpoint.

logo
A unique symbol or design used by organizations to identify themselves.

mailshot
The posting of advertising material to a lot of selected people at the same time.

manipulation
An underhand attempt to influence an individual or group for one's own advantage.

media relations
The art of forming relationships with journalists and publications in order to secure media coverage.

media statement
A written response to a media enquiry – sometimes issued in place of fielding a spokesperson to answer questions – when an organization is unable or unwilling to do a media interview.

photocall
An organization's attempt to attract publicity by inviting newspaper photographers and television crews to attend a staged newsworthy event or 'photo opportunity'. They are encouraged to take pictures for publication or broadcast.

press officer
An in-house specialist in a PR department who issues press releases and deals with media enquiries.

press release
A news story written by PR people in newspaper style and issued to the media by companies and organizations seeking positive press or broadcast coverage.

propaganda
The deliberate presentation of biased information in order to mislead and promote a particular religious, nationalist, or political doctrine. It may avoid the full truth, or falsify or distort the facts in order to achieve this.

regulate
Control, direct, or govern.

reporter
Newspapers and magazines employ general reporters who write about a very wide range of issues. Their correspondents specialize in an area such as education, lifestyle, or crime.

reputation
The general estimation in which a person or organization is held by the public. PR is used to build a good reputation.

slogan
A short, memorable catchphrase.

soundbite
A concise, newsworthy comment taken from a longer media interview which can stand alone from the rest of the interview if necessary.

spin doctor
A PR adviser who puts a positive gloss on the words or actions of an organization or political party. They do this in order to encourage a favourable interpretation.

stakeholder
Someone with an interest in an organization, such as an employee or an investor.

strategy
A plan that sets out tactics that will be used to reach a particular objective or outcome.

sucks sites
Unofficial websites set up by disgruntled customers to air their negative views about a company or organization.

theorist
A person who forms a theory.

theory
A well-substantiated explanation.

Third World
Originally a Cold War term referring to nations not aligned to the USA or the Soviet Union. Now a term for developing nations.

trade press
Newspapers or magazines that publish only information and news relating to a particular industry.

unique selling proposition (USP)
A marketing term used to label a particular feature of a product. The term describes the feature in such a way that makes the product different from other products in a positive way.

whitewash
A deliberate attempt to conceal flaws or failures in order to make something unacceptable appear acceptable.

Books

Bernays, Edward L., *Crystallizing Public Opinion* (1923)

Bernays, Edward L.,*The Engineering of Consent* (1947)

Bernays, Edward L.,*Propaganda* (1928, reprinted 2004)

Christian Aid, *"Behind the Mask"* (2004)

Nader, Ralph, *Unsafe at Any Speed* (1965)

Packard, Vance, *The Hidden Persuaders* (1957)

Ries, Al & Ries, Laura, *The Fall of Advertising and the Rise of* PR (2004)

Theaker, Alison, *The Public Relations Handbook* (2nd edn, 2004)

Websites

There are many organizations across Europe and North America that represent the PR industry and the people working in it. These professional bodies have a code of conduct, which members must follow, and they offer training to help practitioners developtheir skills and expertise. The principal ones are:

The Institute of Public Relations
The largest public relations institute in Europe, the United Kingdom's IPR has 7,500 members. It is organized into specialist groups representing, for example, freelance practitioners, people specializing in healthcare PR, or those working in local government. It also has geographic groups, such as Wales, or the North of England.
www.ipr.org.uk

The Public Relations Society of America
This is the world's largest professional organization for public relations practitioners, with nearly 20,000 members organized into 116 chapters representing business and industry, PR firms, government, associations, hospitals, schools, professional services firms, and non-profit organizations/charities.
www.prsa.org

The Canadian Public Relations Society
Split into 17 member societies, the CPRS does similar work to the IPR and PRSA in Canada.
www.cprs.ca

The Public Relations Institute of Australia
The Public Relations Institute of Australia (PRIA) was founded in 1949 to represent the interests of Australian public relations practitioners and to further the stature of the PR profession.
www.pria.com.au

The Institute of Public Relations of Singapore
Founded in 1970, the IPRS has around 500 members.
www.iprs.org.sg

The European Public Relations Confederation
This umbrella body was founded in 1959 and represents the various European PR bodies.
www.prineurope.com

Titles in the *Influence and Persuasion* series include:

Hardback 0431098328

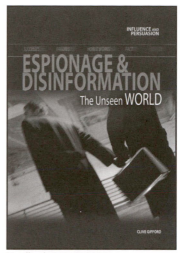

Hardback 0431098336

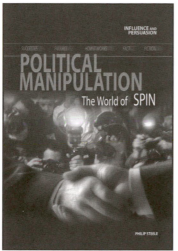

Hardback 0431098344

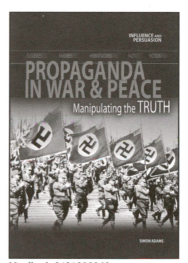

Hardback 0431098360

Hardback 0431098352

Find out about the other titles in this series on our website www.heinemann.co.uk/library